Art & More

Art is what you can get away with.

-Andy Warhol-

www.ingramcontent.com/pod-product-compliance
Lightning Source LLC
Chambersburg PA
CBHW071216220526
45468CB00002B/628
* 9 7 8 1 9 8 3 6 1 9 9 3 9 *